This journal belongs to

_____

Come To Me

JOURNAL

BELLE
CITY
GIFTS

Belle City Gifts
Racine, Wisconsin, USA

Belle City Gifts is an imprint of BroadStreet Publishing Group LLC.
Broadstreetpublishing.com

Come to Me
© 2015 by Renee Swope

ISBN 978-1-4245-5159-0

Design by Chris Garborg | www.garborgdesign.com
Editorial services by Michelle Winger | www.literallyprecise.com

Printed in China.

15   16   17   18   19   20   21   7   6   5   4   3   2   1

"Come to me, all you who are weary and burdened, and I will give you rest."

MATTHEW 11:28 NIV

From My Heart to Yours

Come to me: three simple words extending a powerful and personal invitation from the one who knows you best and loves you most! As I read these words, I picture God with arms open wide, inviting you and me to come to Him to receive and be renewed.

In His presence we find a resting place for our restless hearts, our anxious thoughts, our depleted souls, and our exhausted bodies. But God can only give us what we need if we are willing to come to Him and receive.

Let's draw near to him together as we slow down and let God love us through the gift of his promises, his peace, and his perspective each day. May you be renewed with hope as you reflect through reading and journaling, and then strengthened through a prayer as you are reminded that God is for you and he is with you, no matter what.

Renee Swope

"I will not abandon you as orphans—I will come to you."

JOHN 14:18 NLT

Thank you, Lord, for your promise to never leave me.
Thank you that you always come for me because you desire to be with me.

"Come to me, all you that are weary and are carrying heavy burdens, and I will give you rest."

MATTHEW 11:28 NRSV

Lord, I come to you today feeling weary.
Thank you for offering a resting place where I can give you
the burdens I'm carrying that are too big for me.

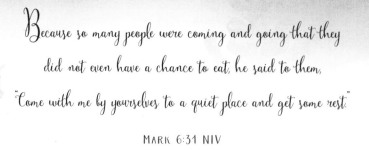

Because so many people were coming and going that they
did not even have a chance to eat, he said to them,
"Come with me by yourselves to a quiet place and get some rest."

MARK 6:31 NIV

Lord, with so many needs around me, I need your help balancing being there for others with my need to be alone with you.

Let us come boldly to the throne of our gracious God. There we will receive his mercy, and we will find grace to help us when we need it most.

HEBREWS 4:16 NLT

Jesus, thank you for inviting me to come to you with confidence, knowing I'll find mercy and grace to help me when I need it most.

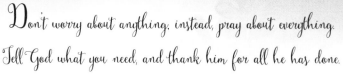

Don't worry about anything; instead, pray about everything.
Tell God what you need, and thank him for all he has done.

PHILIPPIANS 4:6 NLT

When worry comes, Lord, help me remember to pause and tell you what
I need, then thank you for what you've already done in the past.
I want to remind my heart of how good you are at being God.

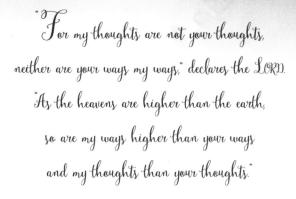

"For my thoughts are not your thoughts,
neither are your ways my ways," declares the LORD.
"As the heavens are higher than the earth,
so are my ways higher than your ways
and my thoughts than your thoughts."

ISAIAH 55:8-9 NIV

Lord, my heart is out of focus and my thoughts are off track;
please reshape my perspective with yours.

Faith is the substance of things hoped for, the evidence of things not seen.

HEBREWS 11:1 NKJV

Just like the wind, although I can't see you, God,
I can feel your presence and know you are with me.

Teach me to do what you want, because you are my God.

Let your good Spirit lead me on level ground.

PSALM 143:10 NCV

Lord, you are my God, and I want to do what pleases you.
I pray that your presence would lead me today and every day.

"Behold, God is my salvation,
I will trust and not be afraid,
For the LORD God is my strength and song,
And He has become my salvation."

ISAIAH 12:2 NASB

Lord, you are my God. I want to trust you as my strength and salvation in every situation I face and decision I make.

Do not be conformed to this world, but be transformed by the renewing of your minds, so that you may discern what is the will of God—what is good and acceptable and perfect.

ROMANS 12:2 NRSV

Lord, I come to you today inviting you to transform my thoughts with the wisdom of yours. I want to be conformed to the pattern of your purpose and perfect will for me.

We have known and believed the love that God has for us. God is love, and he who abides in love abides in God, and God in him.

1 JOHN 4:16 NKJV

LORD, give me courage to Rely on your love more than I Rely on others' approval and acceptance.

The LORD's lovingkindnesses indeed never cease,

For His compassions never fail.

They are new every morning;

Great is Your faithfulness.

LAMENTATIONS 3:22-23 NASB

Lord, thank you for your love that never fails and your
compassion that is new every morning. Not just my good
mornings or mornings that follow good days, but every single
morning. Your faithfulness is more than I deserve.

"You shall know the truth, and the truth shall make you free."

JOHN 8:32 NKJV

Your truth is the only thing that can set me free from worry and doubt. Show me in your Word how to see my circumstances through your perspective today.

One thing I ask from the LORD, this only do I seek:

that I may dwell in the house of the LORD all the days of my life,

to gaze on the beauty of the LORD and to seek him in his temple.

PSALM 27:4 NIV

Lord, help me slow down and savor each moment with you.
I want to live an unhurried life.

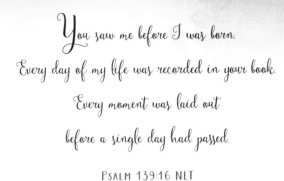

You saw me before I was born.

Every day of my life was recorded in your book.

Every moment was laid out

before a single day had passed.

PSALM 139:16 NLT

God, every breath is a gift from you. You knew me before you formed me
and recorded each day of my life before they came to be.

Cease striving and know that I am God.

I will be exalted among the nations,

I will be exalted in the earth.

PSALM 46:10 NASB

Lord, help me to stop striving. I want to let you be God in my life and in the lives of those around me.

"Peace I leave with you, my peace I give you. I do not give to you as the world gives. Do not let your hearts be troubled and do not be afraid."

JOHN 14:27 NIV

Lord, help me receive your peace with open hands.
When my heart feels troubled, help me put my trust in you.

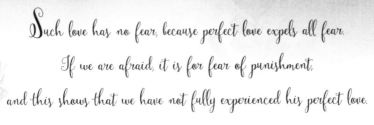

Such love has no fear, because perfect love expels all fear.
If we are afraid, it is for fear of punishment,
and this shows that we have not fully experienced his perfect love.

1 JOHN 4:18 NLT

Lord, help me get off the roller coaster of performance and remember you love me no matter what. Set me free from the fear of what others think by making my heart secure in your perfect love.

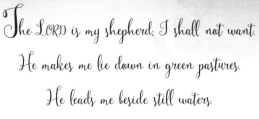

The LORD is my shepherd, I shall not want.

He makes me lie down in green pastures.

He leads me beside still waters.

PSALM 23:1-2 NIV

Lord, you are my shepherd. You do not leave me wanting. Show me the green pastures in my life where you want me to slow down and rest.

Put on the whole armor of God,

so that you may be able to stand against the wiles of the devil.

EPHESIANS 6:11 NRSV

Lord, some days feel like a NON-stop battle. Help me to remember to put on YOUR full armor each morning so I can stand against the enemy's schemes.

He reached down from heaven and rescued me;

he drew me out of deep waters.

Psalm 18:16 NLT

Lord, thank you for reaching down from heaven and holding my hand. Sometimes I feel like I'm drowning in my circumstances and need you to rescue me.

I will say of the LORD,
"He is my refuge and my fortress,
my God, in whom I trust."

PSALM 91:2 NIV

Lord, you are my refuge and my strength. I trust in you, my God.

*He gives strength to the weary
and increases the power of the weak.*

ISAIAH 40:29 NIV

Lord, thank you for providing strength when I am weary and power when I am weak. I come to you today needing both.

"My Presence will go with you, and I will give you rest."

EXODUS 33:14 NIV

Lord, I don't want to go anywhere unless you go with me. In your presence, my heart and soul can rest and be renewed.

*You will keep in perfect peace
those whose minds are steadfast,
because they trust in you.*

ISAIAH 26:3 NIV

Lord, I want to experience the power of your promise to keep my heart in perfect peace when my mind chooses to trust in you alone.

See, I am doing a new thing!

Now it springs up; do you not perceive it?

I am making a way in the wilderness

and streams in the wasteland.

ISAIAH 43:19 NIV

Lord, my soul feels parched and dry like a desert.
Will you bring streams of your living water and do a
new thing in me? I am waiting and watching for you.

I pray that God, the source of hope, will fill you completely with joy and peace because you trust in him. Then you will overflow with confident hope through the power of the Holy Spirit.

ROMANS 15:13 NLT

Thank you for being the God of all hope who fills
me with joy and peace as I trust in you.

Clothe yourselves with compassion, kindness, humility, gentleness and patience.

COLOSSIANS 3:12 NIV

Before I choose something to wear each day,
Lord, help me put on your compassion, kindness,
humility, gentleness, and patience.

Look to the LORD and his strength;

seek his face always.

1 CHRONICLES 16:11 NIV

On my own, I'm overwhelmed, confused, and torn in a million directions. By his side, I am led.

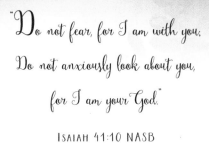

"Do not fear, for I am with you;
Do not anxiously look about you,
for I am your God."

ISAIAH 41:10 NASB

_____
_____
_____
_____
_____
_____
_____
_____
_____
_____
_____
_____
_____

Instead of looking at circumstances around me,
I will focus on and trust my God, who is with me.

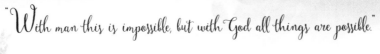

"With man this is impossible, but with God all things are possible."

MATTHEW 19:26 ESV

WHEN I believe all things are possible with you, God,
hope wins every time.

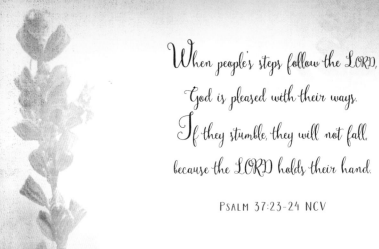

When people's steps follow the LORD,
God is pleased with their ways.
If they stumble, they will not fall,
because the LORD holds their hand.

PSALM 37:23-24 NCV

Instead of giving in, God, please empower me to get up again.

I have set the LORD always before me.

Because He is at my right hand,

I shall not be moved.

PSALM 16:8 NKJV

God, you are before me. You are beside me.
You are always with me. Help me not to be
moved by circumstances around me.

If I rise on the wings of the dawn,

if I settle on the far side of the sea,

even there your hand will guide me,

your right hand will hold me fast.

PSALM 139:8-10 NIV

Lord, thank you for always being there for me.
No matter where I go, you are with me.

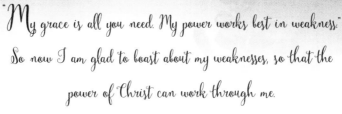

"My grace is all you need. My power works best in weakness."
So now I am glad to boast about my weaknesses, so that the
power of Christ can work through me.

2 CORINTHIANS 12:9 NLT

I can't do it all, Lord. I need your strength to fill in the gaps of my weakness. Help me rely on you more.

"Whoever follows me will never walk in darkness,
but will have the light of life."

JOHN 8:12 NIV

Lord, I want to walk in the light of your truth. Lead me
with the lamp of your Word and be a light for my path.

Faith comes from hearing, and hearing by the word of Christ.

ROMANS 10:17 NASB

God, by reading your Word out loud every day, I can
starve my fears and feed my faith. Help me to do that!

I prayed to the LORD, and he answered me.

He freed me from all my fears.

PSALM 34:4 NLT

Lord, help me to not only believe in you but to really believe you. I want to live like your promises are true, no matter what my fears and feelings tell me.

I am certain that God, who began the good work within you, will continue his work until it is finally finished on the day when Christ Jesus returns.

PHILIPPIANS 1:6 NLT

Jesus, please complete the work you have started in me!

"The LORD your God is living among you.
He is a mighty savior.
He will take delight in you with gladness.
With his love, he will calm all your fears.
He will rejoice over you with joyful songs."

ZEPHANIAH 3:17 NLT

Heavenly Father, you love to watch over me—not because I am doing anything for you, but simply because I am yours.

The name of the LORD is a strong fortress;
the godly run to him and are safe.

PROVERBS 18:10 NLT

God, you are my strong fortress. You are my hiding place
where I am safe from the storm.

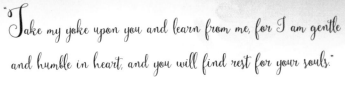

"Take my yoke upon you and learn from me, for I am gentle and humble in heart, and you will find rest for your souls."

MATTHEW 11:29 NIV

Lord, I bend low today so you can remove the yoke of burden that I am allowing to weigh me down. Please replace it with your yoke that is humble and gentle, perfectly fitted for me.

Seek his will in all you do,
and he will show you which path to take.

PROVERBS 3:6 NLT

Lord, I want to seek your will in everything I do and wait
for you to show me which path to take.

Thus says the LORD, who created you, O Jacob,

And He who formed you, O Israel:

"Fear not, for I have redeemed you;

I have called you by your name;

You are mine."

ISAIAH 43:1 NKJV

Lord, I don't have to be afraid. You have
redeemed me and called me by name. I am yours!

In peace I will lie down and sleep,

for you alone, O LORD, will keep me safe.

PSALM 4:8 NLT

Calm my anxious thoughts, Lord. Help me find rest in you.
When concerns keep me awake, help me lay them down at
the foot of the cross and trust my heart with you.

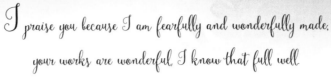

I praise you because I am fearfully and wonderfully made,
your works are wonderful, I know that full well.

PSALM 139:14 NIV

God, I am fearfully and wonderfully made. All of your works are beautiful, and I am one of them.

Set a guard, O LORD, over my mouth;
keep watch over the door of my lips!

PSALM 141:3 ESV

Lord, guard my heart and my words. When I open my mouth to speak, I want to reflect your love and grace.

God is our refuge and strength,
a very present help in trouble.

PSALM 46:1 ESV

God, you are my refuge and strength. You are always
ready to help me. You never leave my side.

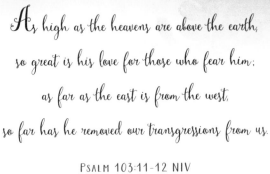

As high as the heavens are above the earth,
so great is his love for those who fear him;
as far as the east is from the west,
so far has he removed our transgressions from us.

PSALM 103:11-12 NIV

God, as high as the heavens are above the earth;
so vast is your love for me!

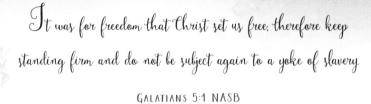

It was for freedom that Christ set us free, therefore keep standing firm and do not be subject again to a yoke of slavery.

GALATIANS 5:1 NASB

It was for freedom that you set me free, Lord. Help me
keep standing firm in the liberty of your grace.

Jesus often slipped away to be alone so he could pray.

LUKE 5:16 NCV

Lord, when everything is pulling on me,
help me remember to pull away with you.

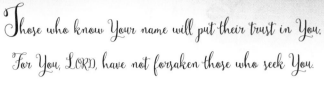

Those who know Your name will put their trust in You;
For You, LORD, have not forsaken those who seek You.

PSALM 9:10 NKJV

Lord, I choose to trust that you will give me what I need, when I need it.

I said to the LORD, "You are my Lord,
I have no good besides You."

PSALM 16:2 NASB

No matter where life takes me, I take this truth with me:
your goodness makes me good enough.

Trust in the LORD with all your heart,

and do not lean on your own understanding.

In all your ways acknowledge him,

and he will make straight your paths.

PROVERBS 3:5-6 ESV

Lord, help me trust you with all my heart, and lean not on my own understanding. In all my ways I will acknowledge you, knowing you will make my paths straight.

If it is possible, as far as it depends on you, live at peace with everyone.

ROMANS 12:18 NIV

God, I know that conflict is inevitable. How I handle it can determine whether a relationship is strengthened or strained. Help me handle all of my relationships with love and grace.

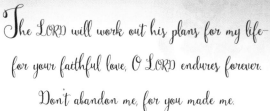

The LORD will work out his plans for my life—
for your faithful love, O LORD, endures forever.
Don't abandon me, for you made me.

PSALM 138:8 NLT

Lord, when criticism comes, help me stay confident in my
calling and grounded in the security of your love.

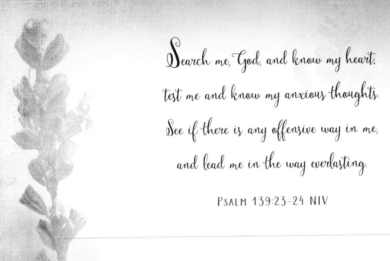

Search me, God, and know my heart;
test me and know my anxious thoughts.
See if there is any offensive way in me,
and lead me in the way everlasting.

PSALM 139:23-24 NIV

God, my conversations with you are more than asking for
you to fix all of my problems. Help me to seek, listen, and
ask you what needs to be fixed in me as well.

Give your burdens to the LORD,
and he will take care of you.
He will not permit the godly to slip and fall.

PSALM 55:22 NLT

Lord, thank you for inviting me to bring my burdens to
you and for promising to take care of me.

You will seek me and find me when you seek me with all your heart.

JEREMIAH 29:13 NIV

God, I know I will find your plan for me when I surrender
my own plans and seek yours each day.

God did not send his Son into the world to condemn the world, but to save the world through him.

JOHN 3:17 NIV

Thank you God, for sending your Son
to rescue me and not to condemn me.

As the deer longs for streams of water,

so I long for you, O God.

PSALM 42:1 NLT

Until your love is enough for me, God,
nothing and no one else ever will be.

No power in the sky above or in the earth below—indeed, nothing in all creation will ever be able to separate us from the love of God that is revealed in Christ Jesus our Lord.

ROMANS 8:39 NLT

Sometimes, God, I just need to be reminded that no matter what, nothing in all creation will ever be able to separate me from your love.

May our Lord Jesus Christ himself, and God our Father, who loved us and gave us eternal comfort and good hope through grace, comfort your hearts and establish them in every good work and word.

2 Thessalonians 2:16-17 ESV

Lord, fill my heart with confident hope as I trust you to establish the work of my hands in everything I do today.

You are a holy people, who belong to the LORD your God. Of all the people on earth, the LORD your God has chosen you to be his own special treasure.

DEUTERONOMY 7:6 NLT

God, I am your special treasure. I am fully accepted,
uniquely chosen, and completely loved. Thank you.

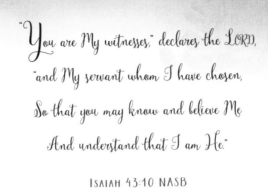

"You are My witnesses," declares the LORD,

"and My servant whom I have chosen,

So that you may know and believe Me

And understand that I am He."

ISAIAH 43:10 NASB

Lord, I am HONORED that you HAVE CHOSEN me to be youR
servant, so I can kNOW you and believe youR pRomises.
I want to kNOW and undeRstand moRe about you each day.

You will go out in joy and be led forth in peace;
the mountains and hills will burst into song before you,
and all the trees of the field will clap their hands.

ISAIAH 55:12 NIV

In every decision I make, Lord, I want to go out
in joy and be led forth with your peace.

Then you will call on me and come and pray to me,

and I will listen to you.

JEREMIAH 29:12 NIV

Lord, I love that I can call on you, and come to you, knowing you will listen to me.

We are God's masterpiece. He has created us anew in Christ Jesus,
so we can do the good things he planned for us long ago.

Ephesians 2:10 NLT

Thank you, God, that I am your masterpiece. I can do all the things you had planned for me from long ago because I am created new in Jesus.

"The Father gives me the people who are mine.

Every one of them will come to me, and I will always accept them."

JOHN 6:37 NCV

_____

_____

_____

_____

_____

_____

_____

_____

_____

_____

_____

_____

_____

_____

_____

Thank you, Jesus, for your unconditional love and acceptance.
Help me choose to get away from everyday life and spend time with you.

Author Bio

Renee Swope is a word-lover, heart-encourager, story-teller, and grace-needer. She's also the best-selling author of the Retailers Choice award-winning book, *A Confident Heart*, with over 150,000 copies sold.

Sharing real-life struggles, rich biblical teaching, and humorous personal stories, through the written and spoken word, Renee offers hope to women and men from every walk by encouraging and equipping them to recognize God's presence, follows his plans, and experience the power of his truth in their everyday lives.

Renee is a national conference speaker and co-host of Proverbs 31 Ministries' international radio program, *Everyday Life with Lysa & Renee*. She's also a contributing writer for Encouragement for Today devotions, DaySpring's {in}Courage blog, and has been featured on BibleGateway.com, Crosswalk.com, and ChristianityToday.com.

Married for over twenty years, Renee is a mom of two grown sons and a daughter they adopted from Ethiopia in 2009 at the age of ten months. For more everyday hope and encouragement, connect with Renee online at www.ReneeSwope.com and on social media: @ReneeSwope.